Reminisc

Confessi

Becky Corwin Adams

BRITTDOG PUBLISHING

Best Wishes,
Becky Corwin-Adams
— 2018 —

Reminiscing About Retail: Confessions of a Cashier
by Becky Corwin-Adams

Published by Brittdog Publishing

Publishers Cataloging In Publication Data Available Upon Request

ISBN: 978-14922424-3-7

Contents

Dedication

This book is dedicated to my mom,
Lois Corwin, who always encouraged me to write.
Mom is also a writer, and I inherited my love
of reading and writing from her.

Introduction

I was born into a family that enjoyed shopping. My mom, grandma, and aunts were always ready to go on a shopping expedition. I loved to shop in downtown Defiance, Ohio, when I was growing up in the '60s. My favorite store was G.C. Murphy's. My older sister Debbie and I played store in our basement when we were growing up. We set up our pretend store on some old green shelves and took turns working at the store.

The day I celebrated my 16th birthday in 1973, I applied for a job at Murphy's. I was hired a few weeks later. I enjoyed working at Murphy's so much that it didn't even seem like work. I worked at the store for almost two years, until I got married and moved away from Defiance.

After living in Minot, North Dakota, for four years as a young Air Force wife, I moved back to Bryan, Ohio, in 1979. Retail was in my blood, so I soon decided to go back to work. I had always thought I would go back to work at Murphy's someday, but by 1979, most of the Murphy's stores had closed, and new Murphy's Marts had been built to replace the smaller dime stores.

We lived very close to Kmart in Bryan. The store was just a short walk across the field near our house. I applied for a job at Kmart and was soon hired, since I had previous retail experience. Although I took a few years off when my sons were young, I worked at Kmart for a total of 17 years.

All of the stores I worked at—Murphy's and two Kmart stores in Bryan—ended up closing. The last store I worked at was Kmart #3960, and it closed on May 24, 2009. The stores may be gone, but the great memories will always be with me.

Downtown Defiance

The Morris 5 Cent to $1 store was located at 416 Clinton Street in Defiance. G.C. Murphy Company purchased the Morris store in the mid-'50s. The Morris store was converted to the G.C. Murphy's store where I shopped as a youngster and worked as a teenager.

Murphy's store #418 in Defiance closed when the new Murphy's Mart opened on the north side of town in 1976. I visited the store during the final liquidation sale and purchased a pair of small milk glass lamps that I still use today. The location is now home to a Mill Direct Carpet and Furniture store.

Hobby Den, owned by Arnold Schilperoot, was a local craft and hobby store located at 302 Clinton Street in downtown Defiance. Many customers complained that employees followed them around the store and made them feel like a criminal if they picked up an item to examine it. I never felt that way, but I was usually accompanied by my mom when I shopped in the store.

Hobby Den sold 45 rpm records and record player needles. The store played the records for customers before they were purchased, to be sure it was the song the customer was looking for if they were unsure of the song title. Hobby Den also sold craft items like beads and macramé cord, which were popular in the early '70s. Some of the store's most popular items included HO slot cars, trains, Matchbox cars, and Barbie dolls. A glass case at the front of the store was filled with Barbie dolls.

Hobby Den is where I bought my Julia doll; she was introduced in the '60s and was one of the first celebrity Barbie dolls. My doll was dressed in a nurse's uniform. *Julia* was a hit TV show that ran for three or four seasons in the late '60s. Diahann Carroll played Julia Baker, a widowed single mom and registered nurse, in one of the first prime time television shows to feature an African American woman.

Woolworth's opened in downtown Defiance in the early '30s in the former Smith Brothers store location at 408 Clinton Street, a few doors down from the Morris store (later G.C. Murphy's). Woolworth's was in business at that location for several decades.

When Woolworth's closed, Lee Henricks opened Stop and Shop at that location. The store sold toys, gift items, and craft supplies. Like Murphy's, Stop and Shop sold candy by the pound from large glass cases.

To prevent shoplifting, one of the salesclerks constantly followed customers around and asked, "May I help you?" multiple times to each customer, which tended to be very annoying.

My friend Joyce and I often went shopping after school. We both liked to crochet "granny" afghans, and we bought a lot of Red Heart yarn at Stop and Shop. The store stocked inexpensive one-ounce skeins of yarn, so we were able to buy a variety of colors on our limited allowances.

A high school friend of mine, Diana Gerdeman, worked at Stop and Shop during the same time I was employed by Murphy's, so we were "retail neighbors." The former Stop and Shop location is now a used furniture store.

Peck's Drug Store in downtown Defiance was located at 300 Clinton Street. The location later became Revco. My mom's lifetime friend, Ruth Grunden, worked at Peck's and Revco for many years. The store eventually moved to the Northtowne Mall. The downtown location is now home of The Fifth Stitch, a yarn and needlecraft store. The former mall storefront is now occupied by Dollar Tree.

Cabbage Patch Kids Dolls were the hot items for the 1983 Christmas season. My sons both wanted one of the popular boy dolls. Mom and I looked everywhere for them with no success. One day we were shopping at Revco and found a

large display of the dolls for $20 each. Fights broke out over the dolls in some stores, and people were reselling them for up to $500.

In the early '30s, Edwin Ruess and Lester Snyder opened The Flower Shop on Clinton Street in downtown Defiance. It later became known as Ruess and Snyder and eventually moved across the street to 323 Clinton Street, the former Standard Store building. Ruess and Snyder closed in 1986 after more than 50 years in business. The building is now occupied by Celebrations, a party store.

My mom loved to shop at JCPenney at 426 Clinton Street in downtown Defiance. Since she didn't drive, Mom walked downtown a couple of times each week to check the clearance rack at Penney's. When my sister was three years old, Mom admired a beautiful little dress in Debbie's size. It was navy blue with white dots. The dress had a pink organdy yoke and underskirts. It was trimmed with white lace and had puffed sleeves. Mom really wanted that dress for Debbie, but it was priced at $15, and she couldn't afford it.

Every time she went to Penney's, Mom checked the girls' department to see if the dress had been sold. One day she saw that it had been marked down to five dollars, but that was still too much money for one dress, so the beautiful little dress stayed there for several more weeks. The next time Mom checked the price, she was pleasantly surprised to see that the dress had been marked down to $3, a price she could afford. Mom bought the dress, along with a pair of pink anklets.

Mom took Debbie's photo in the dress. My sister wore the dress many times, and when she outgrew it, Mom put the dress away. I was born a few years later, and I wore the dress when I was able to fit into it. After I outgrew it, Mom tucked it away again in the closet.

The dress later traveled to New York to be worn by my niece, just long enough to take a few photos. The dress remained in Mom's closet until the late '90s, when my granddaughter and Debbie's granddaughter both wore it and posed for photos. A few years later, the dress was mailed to Alaska to be modeled by Debbie's youngest granddaughter. The dress is still stored away, waiting for the next generation of girls to wear it someday.

Mom and I often walked downtown to shop, even in the winter. One year we went to Penney's a few weeks before Christmas, and she picked up a catalog order. I really wanted a Samantha doll from the television program *Bewitched.* Mom wouldn't tell me what was inside, but the box had a number stamped on the outside. I stared at the number and memorized it as we walked to our house. At home, I grabbed the JCPenney catalog, took it to my bedroom, and looked for the item number. I found out I was getting the Samantha doll, but I acted very surprised when I opened the present on Christmas Eve.

After Murphy's and many of the other downtown stores closed, JCPenney moved to the Northtowne Mall in 1986. The former downtown location is now occupied by Rogliattis Sporting Goods.

The Charles Company

The Charles Company was a chain of northwest Ohio clothing stores that were owned and operated by Edwin S. "Sims" Charles. The first store opened in Napoleon in 1916. The Defiance store opened in 1917 at 402 Clinton Street. In the early '40s, it moved to 312 Clinton Street. At its peak, the Charles Company chain numbered 15 stores in northwest Ohio.

Charles Company sold clothing, fabric, and Boy Scout and Girl Scout uniforms and accessories. When a purchase was made, the money was put into a pneumatic vacuum tube and sent to the office. Many stores used a similar centralized cashier system in the '50s and '60s.

The Bryan location of Charles Company opened in 1926 at 205 South Main Street when Mr. Charles bought a Bryan shoe store and a Montpelier clothing store. He intended to close out the stock of both stores and move the remaining merchandise to his store in Napoleon. The opening sale was so successful that he decided to stay in Bryan and open store number three.

The Bryan store was destroyed by a devastating three-alarm fire in 1932. In 1935, a new building became available at 109 South Main Street, one block south of the former store. In 1945, the basement was dug out to add another floor to the store. The new store was remodeled, and additional departments were added. In the early '50s, the Bryan store was completely remodeled with new fixtures and lighting on all three floors. In 1963, air conditioning was installed.

By 1974, the store had been remodeled again. The basement was devoted to fabric and sewing notions. The street level contained menswear and general merchandise. Women's clothing was located on the second floor. A mezzanine between the first and second floors was opened, for a total of four floors of merchandise. The junior department was on the mezzanine, which was known as "The Loft." The new space was decorated with shag carpeting, spotlighting, and black cedar paneling and beams. The store played popular music for the young shoppers.

Charles Company in Montpelier opened in 1944, at 221 West Main Street; it closed in 1965. After a going-out-of-business sale, the remaining inventory was sold to Glenn McNeilly and the store reopened as McNeilly's Clothing and Shoes.

The Charles Company bought the inventory of the bankrupt McNeilly's at a sheriff's auction a few months later. The store reopened for a short time until the inventory was sold. The former store in Montpelier is now home to Rings Pharmacy.

By the mid-'70s, only four of the 15 stores—the locations in Bryan, Defiance, Napoleon, and Deshler—were still open. The Bryan location closed in 1980, after more than 50 years in downtown Bryan, and Dancer's department store moved in. The storefront is now occupied by Bill's Locker Room III.

The Defiance store closed in the '80s, and Fort Defiance Antiques is now located in the former Charles Company building.

Defiance Stores

In the '6os I walked to school every day with the neighborhood kids. Every day, I had a couple of pennies to buy candy before school.

There were two small stores right by the school—Stone's Market and Snider's Market—both on Clinton Street. My friends and I ran from one store to the other to look at the candy before making a decision. We bought a lot of candy for a few pennies, and on a really good day, when we had a nickel to spend, we bought a full-sized Hershey bar.

Robert Stone and his son, Jim, owned Stone's Market, which was located at 223 North Clinton Street. The location was formerly McLain's store. Stone's Market had a second location on Wilhelm Street.

Gert "Bunny" Harmon, our former West High Street neighbor, was a cashier at Stone's for many years. The most exciting moment in Stone's history was when a student from nearby Defiance College streaked through the store. Stone's closed in 1975, and the North Clinton Street location later became a Carpet Unlimited store.

Snider's Market was located next to Stone's. The store, which was owned by Bill Snider, was very similar to Stone's. We often returned pop bottles to Snider's to collect the five-cent bottle deposit refund. Mr. Snider's daughter, Mary Beth, was a very lucky girl since her dad owned a store that was full of candy. She was my son's teacher at the Bryan Middle School in the '80s.

Discount Stores

Rink's Bargain City opened on North Clinton Street in Defiance in the '70s. For a few years, Kash 'n Karry, a grocery store, was attached to Rink's. The store was not very well maintained, and the ceiling leaked every time it rained. The store was well known for its plastic tarps hanging from the ceiling. Customers had to dodge trash cans that were collecting rainwater in almost every aisle. Check-writing customers at Rink's were subjected to having their photo taken by a cashier with a camera on a wooden tripod.

Rink's also operated a store in Bryan in the 1300 block of South Main Street. After the Rink's stores closed, the Bryan location became a Grant City store.

Grant City opened in 1974 and included a four seasons garden center and lawn supplies department with a separate entrance. The Bryan Grant's store had a snack bar that was well known for its delicious grilled hot dogs. The hot dogs were served on buttered New England style hot dog rolls.

One of Grant's unique features was a small numismatic department, with old coins and supplies for coin collectors. The store also had a large pet department that sold fish, hamsters, birds, and turtles. The Bryan store also featured a complete home improvement and hardware department. A specialty shop for sportsmen included supplies for camping, hunting, golf, tennis, and lawn games.

I remember shopping at the store when I was in high school. Some high school kids I knew used to go to Grant's to shoplift small items like incense. The short-lived Grant City closed in 1975.

In April of 1976, Murphy's Mart opened in the former Grant City building at 1202 South Main Street in Bryan. The store was a part of the G.C. Murphy Company.

In May of 1976, Murphy's Mart opened in a newly constructed building located at 1500 North Clinton Street in Defiance. In April 1985, Ames acquired Murphy's. Many of the larger Murphy's Marts were rebranded as Ames stores. In 1986, Murphy's Mart in Defiance became Ames Store #605. The store closed in 1997 when the lease was sold to Sears. The same Sears store is now part of the Northtowne Mall.

In 1999, Ames reopened very briefly as store #1174 after Ames purchased the former Hill's store at 1800 North Clinton Street, near the mall. The Defiance location was closed for several weeks during the conversion.

In 1986, the Bryan Murphy's Mart became Ames store #588. The store closed in 1993 and was bulldozed so the lot could be used to build a Walmart. Kmart had built a new store across the street from Ames in 1991.

I still remember some of Ames' many slogans from the early '80s: "Amazing Ames," "It pays to shop at Ames," and "Bargains by the bagful." I have an Ames shirt with the "Bargains by the bagful" slogan on the front.

Ames offered a "55 Gold Card" for shoppers age 55 and older. The card entitled customers to a 10 percent discount on all merchandise, including sale items, every Tuesday, at every Ames store. My parents enjoyed using their Ames discount.

Hill's reopened at the 1800 North Clinton Street location as store #174 in the early '90s. Their motto was "Hill's is where the toys are." The store's large year-round selection of toys distinguished the chain from the bigger discounters, which tended to carry only minimal toys except during the holiday season. An entire toy aisle was devoted to Barbie dolls.

I loved the pet department at Hill's, and I purchased a nice leash there for Brittany, my first cocker spaniel. The leash said, "I love my cocker spaniel." Brittany chewed the leash in half a few weeks later, and I didn't love her very much at that moment.

Hill's limited their inventory to a few hardline items, such as basic batteries, paint, and appliances and left the other hardlines to their bigger rivals. Fifty percent of their sales were in clothing and softlines. Hill's stocked their own private label of women's and children's apparel; it was known as American Spirit.

T.G. & Y. Family Center store was located at 1834 East Second Street in Defiance. I can still remember their radio jingle: "Your best buy is at T.G. & Y."

The Defiance T.G. & Y. building later became Quality Farm and Fleet. A few years later, the location became a Big Lots store and a church, Family Christian Center. Big Lots closed in August of 2013.

Downtown Montpelier

Trautman's 5 & 10 Store was located at 314 West Main Street in downtown Montpelier. The store opened in 1924 when Joy Trautman purchased the B. E. Lamont Fair Store at 318 West Main Street. In 1942, the store moved into the former location of Robinson's Meat Market and Augustine's Grocery at 316 West Main Street. In 1946, Trautman's son James went into partnership with his father after returning from military service at the end of World War II.

In 1951, the store was expanded when Trautman acquired the former Miller-Jones Shoe Store building at 314 West Main Street. In 1974, Trautman's marked fifty years in downtown Montpelier. In July of 1987, a going-out-of-business sale started, and the store closed on August 5, 1987 after 53 years of operation.

The store was known for its squeaky, wooden floors that seemed to go uphill or downhill in some places. The large furnace vents in the wooden floor were scary to walk across. Several large ceiling fans cooled the store during the summer. I shopped at Trautman's for several decades.

Trautman's was a typical five and dime store with a big candy counter where candy was sold by the pound. The store had a bell on the front door to alert employees to customers entering the store. Children flocked to the toy department to look for Barbie dolls and clothing, paper dolls, army figures, 10-cent rubber daggers, and cap guns. Other popular toys included Breyer horses and Johnny West people and horses. Model cars sold for $1.50, and Matchbox cars cost 49 cents.

The store also sold jewelry, fabric, 33 and 78 rpm records, vases, candy dishes, handkerchiefs, artificial flowers, and small glass animals. Buster Brown clothing was sold at Trautman's, and some of the clothing was modeled by boy mannequins. At Christmastime, bubble lights were a popular item at Trautman's.

Wermer's Pet Store, at 206 West Main Street, was just a block away from Trautman's. Debbie and I had a guinea pig we bought at Wermer's Pet Store in the early '60s. We named our new pet Sam, and he lived in a cage in our basement. Alfred Wermer sold the store to his son, Jim, in 1979. Jim was a high school classmate of ours and one of Randy's co-workers at Miller's Super Dollar.

In 1995, Randy and I bought a pair of baby guinea pigs at Wermer's. We named them Bubba and Bridgette. We had planned to breed the pair, but Bubba only lived for a week. Bridgette was actually a male, we later discovered, so we called him Mr. Bridgette. We later bought a female named Bernadette, and the two had one baby. Wermer's closed in 1995, and Exotic Scents, a flower shop, now occupies the building.

Downtown Bryan

Mom, Grandma Etchey, Aunt Millie, and Aunt Shirley loved to shop. They met once a week for a shopping trip, usually in Defiance, Bryan, or Montpelier. During the summer, I was allowed to join them, along with Sheri and Vicky, my younger cousins. I especially enjoyed shopping in Bryan at Murphy's and Newberry's. We often bought lunch at the snack bar at Newberry's.

In 1956, the G.C. Murphy Company opened a store in a new building on the south side of the square in Bryan at

111 West Butler Street. Previously, the business had been located at 104 North Main Street. The new store had a large sales area that included home furnishings.

In 1962, Murphy's expanded to add a second sales floor in the basement. The new space was used for a pet department and additional home furnishings. The store closed in 1976 when Murphy's Mart opened in the former Grant City building on South Main Street. My friend Yvonne worked at Murphy's downtown until 1974 when she was hired at the new Bryan Kmart store.

Buckeye Variety, which included a bakery, opened in August of 1979 at the former Murphy store on West Butler Street. The owners were Burton Hazlett, the former Murphy's manager, and his son, Rick Hazlett. My two young sons loved to shop in the toy department. My youngest son always called the store, "Buckeye Bryan." The store was only open for a year or two. The building was later renovated and turned into county office space.

The J. J. Newberry's store was located at 110 South Main Street in downtown Bryan. The store opened in 1928 in a vacant building once occupied by a bakery. In 1936, the store was expanded to the south.

In 1961, the store expanded to the north where the former Bryan 5 Cent to $1 Store, which closed in 1954, had been located. The Newberry store was completely remodeled with all new fixtures and equipment. The exterior of the store was given a fresh, new look.

A popular addition to the store was the expanded clothing department, which included many new brands.

A snack bar was also added to the store during the 1961 renovation. My favorite item at the snack bar was the grilled cheese sandwich with fries. The waitresses wore white or pastel uniforms with a fan-folded handkerchief pinned at the shoulder.

Newberry's had squeaky hardwood floors, like most variety stores in the '60s. The store sold an odd collection of merchandise, including soap and talcum powder gift sets, can opener cozies, toys, garlic shampoo, calico fabric remnants, potpourri sachets, and flimsy greeting cards. Newberry's sold clothing "seconds," including flawed sweaters with sleeves that were mismatched or too long and $2 misprinted T-shirts. Needlework supplies were popular in the '60s, and a skein of embroidery floss cost only five cents. Every October, the store held an anniversary sale featuring large quantities of merchandise at low prices.

The Newberry's in Bryan was phased out in 1979 because the building was too small to allow growth. The store had already been expanded to the north and the south. The store closed on December 24, 1979 after a long liquidation sale. The building is now the home of City Rentals.

Gorny-Winzeler was a gift shop with locations in Bryan and Montpelier. The Montpelier store opened in 1959 in the former Paramount Theater at 218 West Main Street. The store was owned by John Gorny. In 1983, the Montpelier location was sold to Kenneth and Kay Donaldson and reopened for a few years as Wishing Well Gift Shop.

The Bryan Gorny-Winzeler store was originally located on South Main Street. After a fire in 1948, the store moved to 110 South Lynn Street. The gift and office supply store featured a selection of unusual items that shoppers couldn't find in other communities. My favorite part of the store was Toyland on the second floor. The Bryan store was purchased by Special Occasions in 2010.

The Gamble's store in Defiance was located at 216 Clinton Street. The store opened in the early '40s in the former Elite Theatre location. Gamble's stores carried sporting goods, appliances, and toys. Coronado was a popular store brand of electronics sold by Gambles. The line included radios and televisions. Gambles also sold Hiawatha bicycles. The building is now the location of Video Game Trade.

The Gamble's store in Bryan, owned by Ben Chapman, was located at 145 South Main Street. The store closed in the '80s, and Radio Shack moved into the building. The location is now the home of Cornerstone Critters.

Mode O'Day ladies' clothing store in downtown Bryan was located at 105 West Butler Street. Dottie Dotterer managed Mode O'Day for many years, until she became one of my co-workers at Kmart. The location is now occupied by The Bees Knees, a vintage and handmade boutique.

Gamble's and Mode O'Day were part of the Gamble-Skogmo store chain. For many years, I thought Gamble's was just a local store. I later learned that it was part of a national chain that also included Tempo Discount stores and Red Owl grocery stores. I shopped at both of those stores when we lived in North Dakota.

JCPenney's catalog store was located at 141 West Butler Street in Bryan. I often picked up orders from the store, until it closed in 2003.

Downtown Hicksville

The Barr Company was a variety store in downtown Hicksville, located at 115 East High Street. The store was formerly Mentzer's Five and Dime. The store sold candy, salted peanuts, ice cream, toys, hosiery, enamelware, chinaware, and glassware. Mentzer's became the Barr Company in the early '50s.

I remember shopping in this store when I was growing up. Grandma Etchey lived in Hicksville, and we often went shopping when we visited her. The toy department and the candy counter are the parts of the store I remember the most. The toy department was added on to the back of the store in the '60s. Family Dollar now occupies the former Barr Company building.

Childhood Murphy's Memories

Some of my earliest memories of growing up in Defiance in the '60s involved shopping, since Mom loved to shop. She was always looking for a good bargain, and we often walked downtown, since Mom didn't drive at that time. One of my favorite stores was G.C. Murphy's. Aunt Alice worked there for many years. Our neighbor, Evelyn Grube, was a bookkeeper at Murphy's before she went to work at a bank.

Murphy's was a typical five and dime store, and many items were only 10 cents. Murphy's was known as "The

Friendly Store." One of my favorite parts of the store was the candy counter, where you could buy a lot of candy for a dime.

Mom bought a nativity set at Murphy's, one piece at a time, as she could afford it. Each piece had the price stamped on the bottom, and most of them were 29 cents. I still have my Murphy's nativity set.

Debbie and I bought our Valentine cards at Murphy's. We were required to give one to every child in our class so that no one would feel left out. It was fun to read all of the Valentines from my friends, and I kept all of my Valentine cards from elementary school in a box in the basement.

Murphy's had a large pet department with fish, birds, and small animals, like hamsters and guinea pigs. At Easter time, they sold live rabbits, ducks, and chicks as pets. The rabbits were sold for $2.99 each.

The "peeps" were sometimes dyed in pastel Easter colors. The ducks especially were smelly, noisy, and filthy. Although most people did not realize it at first, the chicks were always male, since farmers would not sell hens to Murphy's. The "peeps" became ornery, noisy roosters who were usually given to farmers, sold to poultry markets, or slaughtered in backyards.

When I was eight years old, Debbie and I talked Mom into buying two Easter chicks. Debbie's chick, Chirpy, only lived for one week. My chick, Cheepy, grew into a rooster and crowed every morning. Dad built a pen in the garage for him, but Cheepy finally had to go live on Grandma Corwin's farm, since Dad was afraid the neighbors would complain about the crowing.

Cheepy soon became very mean, and Grandma had to hit him with a rubber hose so that she could get into the chicken coop each morning. Cheepy went to live on another farm with one of Dad's co-workers, and although I begged to visit him, I was never allowed, so I assumed Cheepy was served for Sunday dinner.

Murphy's stopped selling "peeps" in the late '60s because of stricter laws about animal cruelty and the keeping of livestock in stores in the city. I believe Debbie and I got our "peeps" the last year they were sold at Murphy's.

Like most mothers in the '60s, my mom was a stay-at-home mom. One spring, Aunt Alice asked Mom if she wanted a temporary job at Murphy's, assembling Easter baskets. Mom filled the Easter baskets with candy and small toys and covered them with clear cellophane. Toy wooden paddles with attached red rubber balls were also decorated with candy and small toys and wrapped in cellophane.

Mom worked in the stockroom at Murphy's during the summer. Debbie and I had a lot of fun while Mom was working, and she ended up quitting the job because we were having too much fun. Debbie and I ordered pizzas to be delivered to people we didn't even know, after we found their names and addresses in the telephone directory.

When Debbie turned 16, she started working at Murphy's. Aunt Alice's daughter, Gloria, already worked there, since she was a few months older than Debbie. Murphy's allowed employees to make purchases and charge them against their paychecks. Debbie loved to sew, so she bought yards and yards of fabric and charged it. She rarely got a paycheck, since she had spent it several weeks in advance. Debbie and Gloria worked at Murphy's until they started college.

I Was a Murphy's Girl

When I turned 16, Mom asked what I wanted to do for my birthday. I said I wanted to go to Murphy's and fill out a job application. Mom drove me downtown, and a few weeks later, I had a job. I was excited about my first job and looked forward to making $1.20 an hour. Aunt Alice, my cousin Sheila, and Ruth, my cousin Jerry's wife, all worked at Murphy's at that time.

The high school girls ran the store in the evenings after school, and we had a great time. One evening, a man wearing a long black trench coat came into the store and exposed himself to one of the girls. She had to go to the police station to file a report.

I worked in almost every area of the store. I was a cashier, and then a floor supervisor, at the age of 16. There was a checkout counter at both of the store's entrances, and when the cashier needed change, she called out, "Station 2A," and the floor supervisor brought change. If a cashier had a long line of customers, she called out, "Station 2B," and another cashier came to help out. There were two floor supervisors, one for the front of the store and one for the back.

Murphy's experimented with "quick service stations" in the late '60s. A cluster of cash registers was located inside a square wooden cage near the toy department. It proved to be unpopular and was discontinued quickly. My sister worked at the station at Christmastime, and it was very frustrating. Customers lined up on all four sides of the counter, and it was difficult to determine who was next in line. Customers often became irate and yelled at the cashier.

I also worked in the transfer office, which was similar to a customer service desk. The employees would leave their purses at the office while they worked. Everyone had a little round tag with a number to identify their purse, and each purse had to be put into the properly numbered cubbyhole. The transfer office employee also answered phone calls, cashed checks, wrote discount and charge slips for employee purchases, and passed out tokens for the restroom. At that time, the restrooms were locked, and customers had to ask for a token to use the restroom or pay 25 cents.

One of the assistant managers brought his two young sons to work with him some evenings, while his wife was working as a waitress at the Tip Top Café, just down the street. On those nights, my duties also included babysitting for a two-year-old and four-year-old—changing diapers and entertaining the little boys all evening.

The PA system was very old, and it had to be turned on and warmed up for about 10 minutes before it would work. The closing announcement was read twice before the store closed. All of the employees waited by the back door, until everyone had clocked out, and then everyone left together. The transfer office employee had to stay behind with the manager and take the money to the safe at the front of the store.

Layaway was very popular, since few customers used credit cards at that time. The service charge for layaway was only $1.00 with a 10% deposit and 90 days to pay off the balance.

When a customer put merchandise on layaway, it was placed in a box, and the box was covered with brown paper. The six-digit layaway number was written on all four sides and both ends of the box. The boxes were put on the dumbwaiter and stored in the basement. Layaway receipts were written by hand and added up without using a calculator. I never liked working in layaway because it was too much work.

During the winter of 1973, a blizzard started very quickly one evening. Within three hours, a foot of snow had fallen, so the manager decided to close the store early. My friend, Deb, and I both called our dads to pick us up from work, but neither could get their car out of the driveway, so Deb and I started walking home. We both lived on the north side of Defiance, so we walked together through the knee-deep snow across the Clinton Street Bridge and finally got home. Dad was still trying to get the car unstuck, so he was glad to see me, even though he didn't think it was a very smart idea to walk home in a blizzard.

I worked in the pet department during the summer, and one very hot day, we were expecting a truck full of live hamsters for a special sale. The truck arrived very late, and all of the hamsters were dead because the truck's cooling unit had malfunctioned.

When customers purchased goldfish, employees placed them in cardboard containers that looked like Chinese food take out cartons. I really didn't like working in the pet department. I could never catch the parakeets when a customer wanted to purchase one because I was afraid of the birds.

I was one of the few high school employees trained to use the key cutting machine and the window shade cutting machine. Customers would sometimes bring in a piece of string and ask for the shade to be cut "this wide." Employees were supposed to be at least 18 years old to use this equipment, but I was allowed to use it, since no one else on the evening shift had been trained to use it. Very long hair was in style then, and one evening, my hair became stuck in the key cutting machine. When I finally got it free, my hair was a few inches shorter on one side than the other—a difference that is visible in my senior photo.

My boyfriend, Randy, stopped at Murphy's on the weekends. We usually went to the Hub Drive-In Theater in Bryan after work, so he picked me up at the store. Randy arrived early and followed me around the store, talking to me as I worked. The manager, Henry Mehall, did not like anyone bothering his employees, so he kicked Randy out of the store. Randy started calling my boss "meatball" behind his back.

In 1974, there was a toilet paper shortage, and customers were only allowed to buy two of the four-roll packages per day. Whenever a shipment of toilet paper arrived, customers grabbed it out of the box before it could be placed on the shelf.

I also worked at the candy counter. I once heard that managers were told to put the cleanest, neatest, and most attractive girls behind the candy counter to increase sales. I don't know how true that was. The assistant manager told me to eat as much candy as I wanted, so I did. The only stipulation was that I had to bend down and pretend to be looking for something under the counter while eating candy so the customers didn't notice. The assistant manager often came up to the candy counter to do some "sampling" while I was working.

There were dozens of glass cases with many different kinds of candy. When a customer asked for candy, the cashier carefully scooped the candy out of the glass case, weighed it on a scale, put it into a small white paper bag, and wrote the price on the bag. The old wooden mechanical cash registers at the candy counter and the snack bar only recorded sales up to $5.99. Larger sales had to be added up and entered in multiple transactions. The cashier had to push down several keys at one time to get the correct price to pop up.

I also worked at the snack bar at Murphy's. The store sold delicious hot beef sandwiches for 50 cents. Another favorite was the submarine sandwiches. The subs were also 50 cents, and there were only two varieties: with onions and without onions. The ad for the subs featured a picture of the sandwich looking like a submarine with a periscope. A large toothpick with an olive on top was stuck in the sandwich featured on the sign.

At night, we had to wrap up the unsold hotdogs. The next morning, they would be reheated on the roller grill and sold, even though they looked like wrinkled old ladies. The leftover popcorn had to be bagged up, and the next morning it was mixed in with a batch of freshly popped corn. Hot cashews and red-skinned peanuts were also sold at Murphy's snack bar.

Pay was handed out on Fridays, and everyone was given cash in a little brown envelope. At Christmastime, we were given a bonus of $5. On a Sunday evening prior to Christmas, the store held a family Christmas night, and family members could get a 10% discount on store merchandise.

Murphy's was one of the only store chains to offer a week of paid vacation to their employees, including part-time employees, after only six months of service.

In the '70s, Murphy's started opening on Sundays, but only from noon until 5 p.m. Employees got paid an extra 40 cents per hour for working on Sundays.

Year-end inventory started the day after Christmas, and it had to be completed by New Year's. Easter preparation started right after New Year's.

Leakage was the term for merchandise that was lost to thieves or damaged and unsellable. Murphy's Security Department was known as "leakage control."

Murphy's Merchandise

Murphy's stores had wooden floors that squeaked and mahogany counters with glass dividers. The glass was often jagged and sharp from years of use. Extra merchandise was kept behind sliding doors under the counters and was called "understock."

The store windows were decorated weekly with eye-catching displays of merchandise. The person in charge of the displays was referred to as the "window dresser." My store had four large windows, since the store had a front entrance and a side entrance.

Murphy's had more than a dozen private label brands, including Big Murph menswear, Carolina Moon hosiery, Super Tex paint, Pelham men's and boys' clothing, Murtag men's shirts, Murfimade lingerie, Patti Jo girls' clothing, Carole Joanne ladies' shoes, and Regal facial tissue.

In the toy department, you could buy toy soldiers, Barbie dolls, G. I. Joe figures, Colorforms, paper dolls, and Mr. Potato Head sets.

In the mid-'50s, the Murphy's chain was the first retailer to sell the popular new Wooly Willy drawing toy. The toy was not complicated. A round-faced man named Willy was featured as a bald-headed character on a piece of heavy cardboard. A rectangular plastic window on the front of the cardboard covered Willy's face. Metal fragments ground from magnets were sealed inside of the plastic. A small magnetic wand fit into a pouch on the front. The wand was used to move the metal fragments around to form hair, eyebrows, and a beard for Willy.

At first, toy buyers refused to take a chance on the Wooly Willy toys. They thought that the idea was poorly conceived and that the toy would not sell. Finally, a Murphy's toy buyer reluctantly ordered a few dozen of the toys and sold them for 29 cents each. Within a matter of days, the toys were sold out, and Murphy's placed an order for 12,000 of them. The second order sold out quickly, and the rest is history. A larger version of the toy, labeled "Dapper Dan the Magnetic Man," was sold for $1. The toys are still sold in stores today, and other characters have been added to Willy's family.

Mr. Potato Head was the first toy to be promoted through television advertising. The toy was first introduced in the early

'50s. The original Mr. Potato Head set included an assortment of plastic facial features (eyes, ears, nose, and mouth) and black felt eyebrows. The sharp, pronged plastic pieces were stuck into real vegetables and would be considered hazardous by today's standards. The set also included some plastic accessories, such as hats and a pipe. Any fruit or vegetable could be used to make a funny character.

Mr. Potato Head soon "married" Mrs. Potato Head, and smaller Potato Head children were later added to the sets. I was the proud owner of one of the early '60s sets, purchased at Murphy's. Mine featured Styrofoam potato forms that deteriorated rapidly after repeated use. By the mid-'60s, the Potato Head family set was sold with "new and improved" plastic potato-shaped bodies with slots for the plastic accessories.

Murphy's low prices attracted many customers shopping for seasonal items. Collegeville Halloween costumes were sold at Murphy's and were very popular in the '60s and '70s. I usually bought my Halloween costume at Murphy's. Some of the popular costumes in the '60s included Casper the Ghost, Bozo the Clown, Bugs Bunny, Woody Woodpecker, and Porky Pig. Mom purchased the Casper and Bugs Bunny costumes for me.

Murphy's had a mechanical pony ride near the back door, and rides were 10 cents each. I enjoyed many pony rides at Murphy's during my childhood. As a Murphy's employee, I would sometimes sit on the pony while waiting for one of my parents to give me a ride home after my shift ended.

During the summer, Murphy's had an Old Fashioned Bargain Days sale. Clearance merchandise was sold on the sidewalk in front of the store. The submarine sandwiches were sold on the front sidewalk at the amazingly low price of three for $1. Most of the other downtown stores also took part in the three-day event.

When I started working at Murphy's in 1973, the best selling items were five-cent candy bars, five-cent greeting cards, cigarettes, panty hose, and yarn. I regularly purchased all of those items, except for the cigarettes.

Shoplifting Stories

I never personally witnessed any shoplifters at Murphy's, but I heard stories from other Murphy's employees. One time a roll of "thank you" stickers was stolen from behind one of the counters. A man put one of those stickers on a china dinnerware set that sold for almost $50. He showed the set with the sticker to the cashier at the register as he walked out the back door.

After checking with the other employees, the manager determined that the man had not paid for the dishes. About an hour later, the man returned with the dinnerware set. He explained that his wife had gotten mad at him for buying it and had told him to return it to the store for a refund. The manager picked up the dinnerware set, accused the man of stealing it, and refused to give a refund. The manager walked down to the basement stockroom with the set. The man said, "But that's mine," as he walked out of the store.

Another time, there was a seven- or eight-year-old milling around the toy department looking for something, so the manager kept an eye on him. Eventually the little boy grabbed a red Radio Flyer Wagon and pulled it around the store. The manager caught up with the little boy and asked where he was going with the wagon. The boy said he was going over to the entertainment center to steal a TV.

One summer evening, a male customer brought a fishing tackle box to the cash register. The box was stuffed with lures and other merchandise. The cashier dumped everything out and started to ring up all of the items. The man looked surprised, so the cashier asked if he wanted all of the merchandise. The man hesitated for a minute and then said, "Yes." The total of the items was almost $200.

A lady hid a 30-gallon trash can under a circle rack of clothing. She put merchandise in her cart and then dumped it into the hidden trash can. A manager noticed what she was doing, so when the can was about half full, he moved it. The lady got a little rattled when she found the trash can one rack over, but she was dumb enough to keep putting merchandise into it. When the can was almost full, the manager stood by the rack. The lady knew she had been found out, so she quickly left the store. The trash can was filled with all kinds of power tools.

Another lady tried to return a dress she had made from fabric she purchased at Murphy's. Her reason: the dress didn't fit.

Mom said that I was a Murphy's shoplifter when I was three or four years old. I saw a book in the toy department that looked just like a favorite book I had at home. Thinking it was my book, I took it home with me. Mom didn't notice until we got home, and we later returned the book to the store. I don't recall the incident at all.

Kmart 9000

Kmart introduced the Group Nine Program in the mid-'70s and started to build smaller stores in rural areas. The new stores were half the size of a regular Kmart and typically located in communities with populations under 20,000.

Kmart 9000 in Bryan was the first "group nine" store and a prototype store for the new program. Bryan was the first small community in the United States to have its own Kmart. The population of Bryan at the time was around 8,000, which was at the low end of the population scale Kmart worked with.

The store opened on August 15, 1974 at 1204 East High Street. It was the first large discount store in the area.

The group nine stores featured most of the departments the larger Kmart stores had. Only the food department, snack bar, bulk delicatessen, and glassware department were missing.

Kmart 9000 had the typical orange stripes on the walls, orange and beige tables and bins, brown checkout lanes, and buzzing neon lighting. Most Kmart stores looked alike in the '70s, and some of the stores were never remodeled, even in the '90s.

The Kmart stores of the '60s and '70s were wider than they were deep. The midway or center aisle was about 15 feet wide, extending from the front entrance to the back of the store. Promotional, seasonal, and clearance items were featured on tables in the midway. The stores had a central checkout area located near the front of the store. Departments with high-ticket items, such as jewelry and cameras, had their own cash register located within the department in an attempt to prevent theft.

Kmart's advertised prices from a 1976 ad in *The Bryan Times* included

- Automotive battery charger, 6 or 12 volt - $6.88

- Wheel alignment - $4.44

- Quaker State Motor Oil - 37 cents per quart

- 7x binoculars - $17.23

- Live songbird or bird cage - $4.96

- Portable record player - $26.47

- Electric heating pad - $1.96

- 4' x 5' wool afghan - $6.66

- Men's sport shirts - $2.66

- Men's no-iron pants - $2.48

- Ginger jar lamp - $7.88

- Men's sport shirts - $5.88

- Focal film - 96 cents

- Suave shampoo - 66 cents

- Men's tube socks - $1.77

- Bedding plants - 44 cents

- Kmart brand spray paint - 57 cents

All of the above items were rung up on the cash register by hand, since scanning of items had not yet been introduced.

My Kmart Days

I started working at Kmart 9000 in Bryan in August of 1979. Although I had two preschool-age sons, I was bored and wanted a part-time job. We lived so close to Kmart that I could easily walk to work.

I started as a cashier at Kmart. While I was in training on a very hot summer day, a rather large lady wearing a sleeveless dress purchased a television. After I rang up her purchase and stated the amount due, she pulled a roll of 20 dollar bills out from under her arm and proceeded to count out $200. She handed me the very soggy, perspiration soaked money. I quickly counted it and shoved it under the till, as I had been trained to do. Phyl, my supervisor, had a few comments to make after the customer left the store. That was the nastiest encounter I ever had during many years as a cashier.

I soon became the manager of the record and tape department, which consisted of both sides of one aisle. My duties included ordering merchandise and keeping the records and tapes in alphabetical order. The tapes were kept in locked cases behind Plexiglas, with holes for customers to stick their hands through to pick up the tapes and look at them.

Every summer, Kmart held a picnic for the employees. The first time I attended the picnic was about one month after I was hired. I won the grand prize in the door prize drawing—a television. The TV was a small, 12-inch, black-and-white model, and we used it in our bedroom for many years.

One of the richest men in town would often come into the store and buy soda pop. He always said pop was not taxable, even though it was. Each time, he argued until the cashier called a manager, and he always purchased the pop without paying the tax. Making a big scene and delaying everyone else in the checkout line to save a few pennies seemed to make him feel really important. In most cases, the customers waiting in line blamed the cashier for being slow, when it was the customer's fault.

At that time, female employees were required to wear turquoise cotton smocks with the Kmart logo. On each cash register was a sticker that read, "Remember TYFSAK" (pronounced tiff-sack)—a reminder to say, "Thank you for shopping at Kmart," to every customer. Sometimes when an employee made a purchase, the cashier would just smile and say "TYFSAK."

Checks had to be approved at the service desk before customers could check out. The proper way to write the Kmart name was with a capital K and a lower case "mart," with no hyphen. The name was often misspelled, and some customers even referred to the chain as "Kmark." As a cashier, I accepted many checks made payable to "Kmark."

Credit card numbers had to be checked in a booklet that listed stolen card numbers. If a number was listed in the book, the credit card had to be retained. I remember that happening only one time at my store. If a cashier recovered a stolen credit card, she received a $25 bounty.

Employees received their pay in cash, in a brown envelope with the tax information handwritten on the outside. The pay envelopes were handed out through a small cash office window in the stockroom. Employees in the electronics department earned a commission on big-ticket items they sold. I never worked in electronics, since those jobs were in high demand and the turnover rate was low.

A group of about 12 gypsies from Illinois robbed the store one evening in 1980. One of the men went to the cash office and knocked on the door. When the office employee opened the door, the man said someone was having a heart attack and needed assistance. When the employee ran out to help, several of the men entered the office and cleaned out the safe. The group, including an infant, got away. They were quickly caught by the Bryan Police, and the following day, a group photo appeared in the local newspaper.

Gypsies frequently traveled around the Midwest to commit robberies. Although no one saw the incident happen, it seemed that another group of gypsies robbed Kmart 3960 more than 10 years later. All of the money came up missing from a locked change drawer at the front checkouts. After that, Kmart stopped using those change drawers.

At least one person was operating a bogus refund scheme to defraud Ohio Kmart stores. The man was arrested in southwest Ohio with a halogen auto bulb, a receipt for the bulb, several copies of the receipt, and a road map with the locations of various Kmart stores highlighted. The man traveled around the state, stopping at various Kmart stores. He would remove a halogen bulb from the shelf, present it at the service desk along with one of the copied receipts, and receive a refund.

The popular Kmart Employee Savings Plan was started in 1989. Employees were allowed to invest up to 16% of their earnings, with the company matching the first 6% at a rate of 50 cents on the dollar. The company's contribution was invested in Kmart stock, which turned out to be a bad thing for many long-time employees when the stock tanked after the first financial crisis of the new millenium.

Art John was the first manager I worked for at Kmart. He was a very small man, but you didn't want to be around when he was angry! Mr. John was the manager for many years. The next manager was Dan Waggoner. He was the first person I knew who owned a car phone, an early version of the cell phone. Dennis Baird was the manager of Kmart 3960 from 1991 until 2007. He is currently manager of a Kmart in Fort Wayne, Indiana.

Kmart was the corporate sponsor of the March of Dimes Walk America for many years. My first year as a member of the Walk America team was very memorable. The event was 25 kilometers, the equivalent of 18 miles. Since Bryan is such a small town, we walked many miles on gravel country roads. I was determined to finish the entire route, unlike many people who quit or cheated by skipping large parts of the trail.

I felt a great sense of accomplishment when I completed the walk. I was planning to go home and put up my aching feet, until one of my younger co-workers called in sick so that she could go to the lake. Being a glutton for punishment, I worked a six-hour shift that evening, after walking 18 miles in less than six hours.

I participated in Walk America seven more times, including one year when I was accompanied by my young granddaughter and her mother. For several years, I was a team captain.

Another benefit walk I participated in was a fundraiser for Angie Mitchell, the daughter of Linda, one of my Kmart co-workers. Angie was born with serious health issues and later underwent a successful five-organ transplant. The five-mile pledge walk raised money to help with medical expenses. Angie worked in the footwear department at Kmart for a few years as a high school student. Angie passed away at the age of 26, and I will never forget her. Serious health issues didn't prevent Angie from driving race cars and owning a menagerie of pets, including birds, dogs, and a horse.

Sporting Goods

I left Kmart in 1981 to stay at home with my sons who were not yet in school. I returned to Kmart in 1985. At the time, the only opening was in the combined sporting goods and automotive department. I didn't really know much about the products, but since it was considered a "specialty" department, I earned 30 cents an hour more than I would have earned as a cashier.

Kmart sold live worms and kept them in a small refrigerator in the sporting goods department. The worms were packaged in plastic containers that looked like cottage cheese cartons. When a customer purchased worms, the container had to be opened to show them that the worms were indeed alive and wriggling.

During hunting season, Kmart sold small glass bottles of doe-in-heat deer scent. Whenever a bottle got dropped and broken, a terrible smell was released, and it lingered for several days.

I sold guns and ammunition, and every purchase had to be logged in a book. One evening a convicted felon attempted to purchase a gun. When I explained that he could not buy the gun because he answered "yes" to the question about being a felon, he became very upset and abusive. He finally left the store after making quite a scene.

In those days, customers only had to complete a simple form and answer a few questions to purchase a gun. It was very easy to get away with lying on the form, since there were no background checks. When a customer purchased a gun, an employee had to carry the gun outside of the store before handing it to the customer.

I learned how to measure, fit, and drill bowling balls. That was not one of my favorite tasks because it was so easy to make a mistake. No one could ever remember which way to turn the screws to secure the ball in the vise, so someone made a sign that read, "Lefty loosey, right tighty" and hung it above the work table. We used a set of alphabet dies and a special tool to stamp the customer's name or initials on the ball. You had to apply just the right amount of pressure or the results were crooked or at an inconsistent depth. The letters were colored in with a special crayon.

We had several department managers in sporting goods, and each of them had annoying habits. Most of them did not think females should be working in the department. Each manager had a "tour book" and they would walk around the department, writing a long list of projects to be completed. We were expected to get everything on the list completed and crossed off by the time the store closed each night.

One of the sporting goods managers had some very strange mannerisms. He often wore torn clothing that he had attempted to patch by sewing on pieces of an old towel. One day he called me into the sporting goods office, and when I opened the door, he had his shirt unbuttoned, and he was applying deodorant. I started to walk out, but he told me to come in, and he talked to me while continuing to apply the deodorant, which he finally placed in a filing cabinet drawer.

After the sporting goods department was downsized, two of the assistant store managers hid their candy in the filing cabinet. Most of the employees knew which drawer contained a five-pound bag of candy. About once a year, the managers would empty the drawer and start the grapefruit diet. Within a month, the stash of candy was back, and life was good at Kmart 9000.

Customer Service Desk

After a few years in sporting goods, I was promoted to customer service. I was responsible for supervising the checkout lanes and working at the service desk. Often, one person was responsible for both of these tasks.

I processed thousands of refunds during my years at Kmart. Many customers lied about items not working if they thought they were going to be denied a refund. Many of these items were tested later and found to be in good working condition. A card file was kept in a drawer with notations about customers who frequently returned items without a receipt. Some of the regular customers had a lengthy file.

One customer returned some Christmas lights that he claimed did not work. That could not be verified, since the irate customer had cut the wires into one inch sections and broken the bulbs into small pieces. He put all of the pieces in a tin Band-Aid box and emptied the contents of the box all over the service desk counter. He did get a refund, and I had to clean up the mess on the counter. I assume the man felt better after taking his frustration out on the string of lights!

Some customers confused Kmart with a rental store. They would wear clothing once and return it, unwashed and obviously worn. People would return tents and other camping equipment at the end of the summer. They had no receipt or box but expected a full refund. A few people were even known to frequent garage sales and buy items to return for a refund. Kmart was forced to become stricter with its refund policies, and many customers got irate when they were refused a refund without a receipt.

One of the cashiers I supervised was an older lady named Betty, who just worked at Kmart for something to do. She always played the lottery. One night at break time, Betty told me she forgot to buy her lottery tickets, so she was going to buy them at a nearby convenience store on her 15-minute break. Leaving the store was a violation of company policy, since 15-minute breaks were taken on the clock. Betty insisted that she didn't care if she got fired because she needed those lottery tickets. I turned my back and didn't watch her leave the store. She returned in less than 15 minutes, happily holding the tickets. To my knowledge, she never did win the lottery.

Answering phone calls was always entertaining. Since there were no cell phones, people would often call the store and ask to have a customer paged. The caller always said it was an emergency. One time, I decided to have some fun. When the customer I paged came to the service desk, I told him there was an emergency phone call. The guy got very pale, and I thought he was going to pass out. After he talked to the caller for a few minutes, I heard him say, "A gallon of milk. Anything else?" It didn't sound like an emergency to me!

Some customers would call and ask for the manager. It was usually a simple question that any employee could have answered. The manager often asked why they were given a certain phone call, so we started screening the calls and asking what information the customer was seeking.

The Simpsons was a very popular television program in the '80s, and one episode involved Bart Simpson calling stores and asking them to page "I. P. Freely" or "Mike Hunt." After several callers had attempted this prank at Kmart, one of the service desk employees finally fell for it and paged "Mike Hunt." She had no idea why everyone in the store was laughing, until someone explained it to her, and then she turned several shades of red.

Another popular question was, "Do you know the phone number for Marco's Pizza?" People expected us to know the phone number, since Marco's was in the same plaza as Kmart. Some callers would ask if a certain item was in stock, and if it wasn't, they would say, "Do you know if Walmart has any?" They didn't realize we had no idea and wouldn't tell them if we did know, since "Walmart" was like a swear word at Kmart.

Kmart Awards

Certificate of Achievement
Outstanding Customer Care

This award acknowledges that

BECKY ADAMS

has been recognized for outstanding performance in

CUSTOMER CARE

JUNE 6, 1990

Richard F Voss
DIRECTOR OF MANAGEMENT TRAINING AND
DEVELOPMENT AND CUSTOMER SERVICE

J. E. Antonini
CHAIRMAN OF THE BOARD

Kmart Corporation

The Kmart Corporation awarded cash bonuses to employees for submitting ideas that saved the company money or made a task easier. I won three Suggestion Awards at Kmart. One suggestion involved increasing the turnover rate of candy bars at the checkouts by placing the slower sellers at the top of the rack. My second award was for suggesting that we fasten the jersey gloves in sporting goods together with Swiftachment fasteners. The third suggestion improved the golf club pricing system by placing a tag with the UPC code and price on the golf club shaft and securing it with clear tape. Prior to that, price tags were placed on the head of the clubs, and the tags always fell off.

I received 12 Kmart Chairman's Awards for outstanding customer care. In the early '90s, we were encouraged to ask customers to call an 800 number if they were happy with the service they received at our store. I was also chosen as Employee of the Month twice. That was a very coveted award because it included a day off with pay.

Kmart had a Good News Committee, which was comprised of employees who were interested in volunteering for community service projects. I was a member of the committee for most of my Kmart years. Some of our projects

included an Easter egg hunt behind the store, selling root beer floats as a fundraiser, and selling paper shoes for the March of Dimes Walk America. As a member of the Good News Committee, I received a Community Volunteer Award for my volunteer service with the Community Pregnancy Center.

I entered a poster contest in 1991, and my poster was chosen as one of 12 winning entries. A copy of each winning poster was displayed in every Kmart store, one each month, for the next year. I kept the poster for many years until it was destroyed during a move to a new house.

Kmart 3960

In 1991, the announcement was made that Kmart 9000 was being replaced with a new store, twice the size of the old store. This new store would be built on the south end of Bryan, across the street from the Ames store, which is now closed. Many of the employees were unhappy about this news. We all realized that our small, close-knit Kmart family was about to expand.

Most of the employees stayed at the old store until it closed for the final time, the day before the grand opening of Kmart 3960, the new store. We had a tailgate party in the parking lot that last evening at Kmart 9000, and it was a very emotional night. Many of the employees had worked at the old store since it opened in 1974.

The new Kmart store opened in November of 1991 at 1120 South Main Street. The store was the main tenant of the new Southtowne Shopping Center. There were about 300 employees at the new store, and the newly hired employees who had set up the store weren't very friendly to us "old-timers."

The new store had a big book department, Reader's Market, and it was one of my favorite departments. The store never had a pharmacy because the lease holder had signed a 10-year non-compete clause with a nearby Rite-Aid Pharmacy. By the end of the 10-year period, there was a Walmart across the street, and Kmart's business was declining, so a pharmacy was out of the question.

For many years, the cafeteria at the new store was a popular gathering place during breakfast hours. Store employees frequently visited the cafe at breaktime. The morning meeting was held every Friday morning at the cafe, and employees and customers received free donuts and coffee. Once a month the employees played Bingo in the cafe for an hour and won small prizes. The cafe also started a monthly Bingo day for senior citizens, which proved to be very popular.

The new store had a large outdoor garden center, and the younger male employees all wanted to work out there, since it was not closely supervised. Often they would go outside to smoke and even drink beer. One of the employees accidentally set the garden center pallets on fire. He decided to put some leftover fireworks inside a stuffed Sesame Street Ernie doll and light it in the parking lot. He didn't think Ernie would travel such a great distance!

Covert Operations

In the early '90s Kmart became obsessed with matching Walmart's prices. Even before Walmart opened across the street from our Kmart, we had to match their prices. I was offered the position of district price checker. I was trained by Debi, an experienced price checker from one of the Toledo stores.

Debi trained me to use a small, easily concealed tape recorder. It was a very challenging task to walk around Walmart and record the prices of hundreds of items without being noticed. Walmart had a sign at the front of the store stating that recording prices was not allowed.

Debi always used a shopping cart and placed random items in it so that she would look like a shopper while she was checking prices. When she finished her work, she took great delight in ditching the cart full of items and walking out of Walmart, laughing all the way to the car.

After each visit to Walmart, I spent hours listening to the tapes and writing down the prices in the office at Kmart. I soon decided that it was easier and faster to write the prices on small pieces of paper, so I stopped using the tape recorder. It was more difficult to write without being noticed, but I was fairly good at it. Sometimes I would look at several prices and then go into the restroom to write them down.

I did get kicked out of Walmart a few times. Walmart had a policy of evicting anyone observed in its stores with a camera or a notepad. Once I was price checking with Jennifer, an apparel manager, and we got caught. The Walmart manager ordered Jennifer to hand over her pen, so she complied by throwing it at the manager. If I got kicked out, I would just go back the next day and finish my task.

As district price checker, I gathered prices for three Kmart stores: the Bryan store, the Wauseon Kmart (a small group nine store like Kmart 9000), and the new Defiance Super Kmart. I often traveled to those stores to drop off price lists. I also did some price checking at the Walmart in Napoleon, and I was kicked out of that store several times, too.

I rarely shopped at Walmart on my personal time, since I was constantly followed around the store because they thought I was checking prices. One of the Walmart assistant managers was my neighbor, and she followed me around the store a lot. If I passed her house when I was walking my dogs, she was very friendly and talkative. I often thought about reminding her that I was the same person she had kicked out of Walmart a few days earlier.

In the early '90s, a year or so after I became the district price checker, the Wauseon Kmart closed. Super Kmart 4903 in Defiance closed in 2008. By that time, the position of district price checker had been eliminated.

Unusual Customer

In October of 2005, an unusual customer visited Super Kmart 4903 in Defiance. A four-point buck walked up to the store's south entrance early one evening. The doors automatically opened as they did for every customer.

The buck jumped over a display of pants and knocked over a rack full of coats as he headed to the men's department. The animal had a difficult time keeping his footing on the slippery tile floor, so he appeared to be ice skating.

As the buck continued on to the furniture department, a customer began to chase him. The buck continued through the automotive and do-it-yourself departments before arriving at the layaway department. The deer jumped over the counter and was trapped in the small layaway area.

The Defiance County Dog Warden was called. He shot the buck with a tranquilizer, which caused the animal to fall to the floor. The dog warden, a Defiance police officer, and a male Kmart employee wrestled with the buck for 20 minutes before they were finally able to tie its feet with rope.

The flailing buck was loaded onto a Kmart flatbed cart, then taken outside and shot by the dog warden because procedures called for killing a deer that had been tranquilized. If a hunter later shot the animal, drug residue from the tranquilizer could pose a hazard if the meat was processed for human consumption.

Deer were a common sight near the Super Kmart, which was located adjacent to a field on the edge of Defiance. The area goes from city to rural behind the Kmart property. When the store had its four-legged visitor, bow season was underway, and the deer was probably seeking a safe haven at Super Kmart.

Claims Clerk

My final position at Kmart was claims clerk/605. The term "605" referred to a form that was used to process returns. All of the damaged merchandise was placed on shelves in my little corner office in the stockroom. My job was to sort the items and process them for credit.

Damaged clothing was sorted into boxes by category: men's, ladies', children's, or accessories. Food items were usually written off as a loss and thrown away. Vendor items, including videos, music CDs, books, and greeting cards, were sorted and placed in bins until the vendor came in to write a credit.

Almost everything else was sent to Genco, the Kmart return center. I scanned each item and boxed everything up. After stacking the boxes and larger items on pallets, I shrink-wrapped and labeled each pallet. The returns were picked up every other week.

Paint was frequently mixed wrong and returned. When I took over the position, there were at least two dozen cans of paint that had been ignored for awhile. The cans had to be opened and set outside until the paint hardened and could be safely disposed of.

My other duties included adding up the refund slips from the previous day and covering breaks at the service desk, layaway, and receiving. I was also the district price checker at the time.

I met a lot of merchandisers, and I often talked to them at length about their jobs. I finally decided to leave Kmart for the third and final time in August of 2001, and I became a merchandiser.

I worked for at least a dozen merchandising companies during the next 12 years, sometimes working for as many as nine companies at the same time. Since the jobs were all part-time, it was easy to combine them. I merchandised a variety of product lines: greeting cards, reading glasses, sunglasses, books, movies, and jewelry. I soon discovered that the grass is not always greener on the other side—merchandising is still retail. I currently work for only one merchandising company. My territory includes almost 60 stores within a 20 mile radius of my home. Only one of the stores is a Kmart store.

Kmart Kapers

Every morning, we were required to gather at the front of the store at 8 a.m. for the morning meeting. At the end of the meeting, we had to do the Kmart cheer:

Give me a K.

Keep those customers coming.

Give me an M.

Maximize sales.

Give me an A.

Always low prices.

Give me an R.

Real value always.

Give me a T.

Together we'll do it.

What does that spell?

KMART! KMART! KMART!

Our first district manager at Kmart 3960 was a man named Jerry. Most of the employees called him "Scary Jerry." Once, while checking out a customer, a cashier told another employee that "Scary Jerry" was in the store. The cashier later found out she was checking out "Scary Jerry's" wife at the time. That was the last time we gave a nickname to our district manager.

I never had a problem with Jerry. I was the district price checker at the time, and he gave me a nickname, too. He always referred to me as "the shining star of the district."

We had a new district manager after Jerry was transferred. As the new manager was being introduced to a service desk employee, she shook his hand and said, "I'm happy to meet you, Mr. Black." There was only one small problem: black was not his name, but his skin color.

One night some bored employees placed a cardboard Tom Selleck in the restroom. Someone later did the same thing with a Jaclyn Smith cardboard figure. There were quite a few startled screams in the restroom when a customer turned the light on.

One year on Halloween eve, we placed a life-sized skeleton in the store cafeteria. An assistant manager named Paul always sat at a table in the corner, which he referred to as his "office." Before the store closed for the night, we dressed the skeleton in a Kmart vest, a hat, and a name badge that said "Paul." We put a cigar in one hand and a can of Dr. Pepper in the other hand. When Paul came in the next morning, he had a good laugh. He said he would probably die while sitting in his office at Kmart and turn into a skeleton before anyone noticed.

Kmart had a Halloween costume contest with nice prizes every year. In the early years, people really got excited about dressing up. One year, the entire office staff dressed as characters from *The Wizard of Oz*. Another year, Yvonne, Sue, and Laura dressed as the popular '70s television characters, The Coneheads. There were always prizes for the best costumes.

An employee named Carol dressed as an outhouse one year. She called her costume "the holes of fame." Carol wore the outhouse costume during our Friday morning meeting. She used a plastic squirt gun to spray water through the holes, hitting the store manager. He kept asking who was inside the outhouse, and no one volunteered to answer the question. Carol also turned on a laughing machine whenever the manager tried to talk during the meeting.

An assistant manager named Rick was quite popular with the female employees, and he was given the nickname "Eveready." No one thought he knew about the nickname until one Halloween when Rick made an Eveready battery costume and wore it to work.

We named our trash compactor "Igor." Marcia, the footwear manager, often volunteered to climb inside to clear jammed trash. Since climbing into the compactor was a violation of company policy for safety reasons, another employee would stand guard to prevent people from pushing the button to start the compactor. One time Marcia climbed around in the compactor to search for the jewelry department keys because someone had accidentally thrown them away.

In 1995, some of the employees decided to enter the Bryan Jubilee Parade as a marching unit. They called themselves "The Kmart Krazy Kart Korp." Each of the twelve team members decorated a shopping cart and pushed it for two miles along the parade route, while performing some fancy maneuvers. My son Casey was a Kart Korp member.

Revitalization Programs

By the early '80s, Kmart had a poor reputation and was best known for its dirty stores and out-of-stock advertised items. Kmart was reluctant to invest in modern technology and struggled with an outdated inventory control system. The existing stores were rundown, the fluorescent lighting was outdated, and merchandise was haphazardly tossed on tables, often still in the shipping carton.

Too late, Kmart began to renovate older stores in an attempt to shed its image as a second-rate bargain basement. Like Walmart, Kmart claimed to have "everyday low prices" on thousands of popular everyday items.

By the end of the decade, Kmart had hired store greeters, in an attempt to copy Walmart's newly implemented "people greeter" program. Most customers would have preferred to have more checkout lanes open. They would rather shop without having someone standing near the front door, smiling and handing them a sale flyer they didn't want, and shoving a cart at them when they only intended to purchase one or two items.

Contracts were signed with Martha Stewart, Jaclyn Smith, Kathy Ireland, and Mario Andretti to promote various product lines. In the late '90s, Kmart introduced a line of brand name home furnishings and accessories known as Martha Stewart Everyday.

Fuzzy Zoeller promoted Kmart merchandise until he was released from his contract after making disparaging comments about Tiger Woods. Zoeller's comments were deemed inappropriate and offensive and were in violation Kmart's strict policies.

In the mid-'90s, Rosie O'Donnell was hired as a Kmart spokeswoman, and she appeared in hundreds of Kmart ads. O'Donnell resigned at the end of her five-year contract, basing the decision on her strong beliefs about gun control. At the time, Kmart still sold guns and rifles in most of its stores.

Kmart finally adapted to the new technology when they invested in computers for inventory control. Kmart started to scan bar codes in the early '80s, forcing suppliers to put a UPC on every product. Walmart and other retailers soon followed Kmart's lead. At the same time, Kmart started using its own distribution centers.

By 1990, Kmart had implemented a three billion dollar renovation program, and the formerly outdated stores took on a pleasing new appearance. The updates included wider aisles and improved lighting. New stores that were built during that decade were larger than the previous stores.

At the same time, Kmart's apparel revitalization program added more fashionable, higher priced apparel items to the store's inventory. The previous apparel line featured poorly constructed private label clothing that often lacked style. More brand name merchandise was added to the mix, including popular Bugle Boy jeans and Seiko watches.

A Kmart program that failed during the revitalization decade was Muttsy, often referred to as the "Kmart dog." The soft, floppy stuffed toy was introduced in 1992 and sold for $7. Kmart purchased 50,000 of the dogs from a company in South Korea.

Gund, Incorporated soon filed a suit against Kmart. The action claimed that the dog was a cheap imitation of a dog from their line of stuffed toys. A judge ruled in favor of Gund, and Kmart was ordered to remove the dogs from its inventory. I wish I had purchased one of the dogs while they were available, but I was not a dog person at the time.

Big Kmart

Kmart introduced the Big Kmart program in the late '90s and changed the name of its stores. The stores were refurbished with fresh paint in a new red and white color scheme, and new outdoor signage featured the Big Kmart logo. The former letter K with the gaudy turquoise "mart" was replaced with a red letter K. The word "mart" was written in script, inside of the letter K. Over 50% of the Kmart stores had been converted to the new Big Kmart concept by 1999.

All stores added a new grocery department. The Pantry occupied a large portion of the center of the store. Several aisles were stocked with groceries, adding about 2,000 items to Kmart's formerly limited line of canned, frozen, and refrigerated foods. The space was taken from other departments in the store. Employees were regularly pulled from other areas of the store to keep the Pantry shelves full. The Pantry concept was intended to increase shopper traffic, hopefully enticing customers to purchase other items while they were picking up groceries.

Over the years, Kmart introduced many new programs, most of which were not very successful. "Blue Lightning" was designed to speed up the checkout process without opening more checkout lanes. Employees were summoned to the front of the store to scan the items in a customer's shopping cart using a handheld scanner or RMU (remote marking unit). Each customer was handed a plastic card to present to the cashier, who scanned the card and completed the sale.

Most of the employees hated the program and preferred to open another checkout lane. The process did not make sense. The items still had to be bagged and payment had to be made, so basically no time was saved.

In 2000, Kmart implemented 10,000 price cuts to match Walmart's prices. The majority of store employees spent many long days putting up new SEM (shelf edge marking) labels. At the same time, small signs called "wobblers" were attached to the shelf near items with reduced prices.

The program was the number one priority for several weeks while other job duties were pushed aside. In another desperate attempt to compete with Walmart, the price cuts were soon increased to include a total of 20,000 items.

At the same time, Kmart changed the name of their cafeterias from "Eatery Express" to "KCafe," and they sold Kmuffins (similar to McDonald's Egg McMuffin) during breakfast hours.

In the '80s and '90s, Kmart sold stuffed holiday bears in several colors. Each bear was marked with the year, and many people bought one or more of the bears every year. The bears were suspended from the ceiling on white plastic chains near the checkout lanes.

The bears were very popular with customers and very irritating for the frontend employees who were kept busy hanging the bears from the chains. If a rolling ladder was not available, employees would stand on the checkout counter to reach a bear for a customer.

The week after Christmas, Kmart held its annual Dollar Days sale, where many items in the store were just one dollar. The sale was very popular, and the store was always busy. Items were often sold out, so we had to handwrite rain checks for customers who requested them.

Everything at Kmart started with a "K." The company newsletter was "The K-liner." The computer system was referred to as KIN (Kmart Information Network). The housewares department was renamed "Kitchen Korner."

Employees who went above and beyond were often rewarded with "Knotes," which could be exchanged for Kmart gift certificates.

Kmart had a slogan, "Over four, call for more," which meant that, if more than four customers were waiting to check out, cashiers would call for assistance. Sometimes, there were no available employees to open another checkout lane, but managers used the PA system to make "phantom calls" in an attempt to keep the customers happy.

Kmart experimented with self-service checkout lanes in 2001. The new self-checkout lanes allowed customers to scan and bag items, then choose their method of payment. The lanes were removed the following year after the lease for the equipment was cancelled. Too many items were never scanned, which contributed to the "shrink" rate. Half of the store's regular checkout lanes had been removed to install the self-service lanes and were never replaced in most stores.

Kmart had a policy of no pallets of merchandise on the sales floor after 10 a.m., so all of the employees had to put freight out first thing every morning. The program was called "all hands on deck." Everyone was supposed to help with the freight. The program never worked because employees were constantly excused from helping, until there was only a handful of employees left to work through a mountain of freight.

Kmart Characters

The parking lot at Kmart 9000 was bordered on one side by a low income apartment complex. A tall chain-link fence separated the two properties. Many of the apartment dwellers were frequent Kmart shoppers, even though they had to walk quite a distance to get to the store because of the fence. Finally, someone cut the fence and made an opening, which was never repaired.

There were some interesting people living in the apartments, and my co-workers and I often saw them walking to Kmart. A new assistant manager was transferred to our store from a larger store in Fort Wayne, Indiana. After a few days, Paul mentioned that there were more strange people in Bryan than the entire city of Fort Wayne, which was considerably larger.

A frequent Kmart customer was a little old man with a bad attitude who almost always wore black. We called the man "Crazy Charlie." He always carried a big wrench in his back pocket. I was afraid he was going to use it as a weapon.

Charlie was the worst customer I ever encountered the entire time I worked as a cashier. He carried his money in a brown paper bag. Charlie talked to his money, and it took forever for him to pay. He turned each dollar bill over and examined it before handing it to the cashier, one bill at a time. An employee once asked why he talked to his money, and he told her it was none of her (expletive) business. It took Charlie forever to leave the store since he always re-bagged his purchases because it wasn't done to his specifications.

Once, Charlie threatened to sue Kmart because he thought a cashier had rung up another customer at the jewelry counter before him. The customer told him she would go to court and testify for the cashier. The discussion got very heated. Another time, Charlie told a 16-year-old cashier that she was a "bad clerk" because she couldn't answer his question about wallets.

On yet another occasion, an employee helped Charlie shop for clothes for his girlfriend for more than two hours. He said he was going to New York City with his girlfriend to break into show business.

One of our store greeters was Beverly, a very friendly and outgoing lady. One day she was wearing a bright, flowered blouse when Charlie came into the store. He started calling her "Bahama Mama," and the nickname stuck for the rest of Bev's Kmart career.

Another greeter was a friendly older man named Al. One time two teenage boys were harassing him, so Al followed them out into the parking lot. He punched one of the boys and ended up getting fired. We were all sorry to see Al go, but happy that the annoying kid got what he deserved.

One of the Kmart greeters was a man named Dennis, who had worked at General Motors with my dad. Dennis worked at Kmart as a retirement job when he wasn't repairing sewing machines and vacuum cleaners at his family business in downtown Bryan.

Julia and Edna were two longtime Kmart greeters. They were both very kind older ladies who were a lot of fun to work with. I later found out that Julia's brother had been married to my aunt in the '50s. Julia and Edna are still good friends today and spend a lot of time together.

BlueLight Specials

Astore manager in Fort Wayne, Indiana, is credited with creating the BlueLight. He instituted the popular program at his store, and it was soon adopted chain-wide.

The original BlueLight Special, first introduced in 1965 as a promotional gimmick, was in use until 1991. Initially, BlueLight Specials were announced every hour, and they lasted for 10 minutes. In its heyday, the flashing blue light was a novelty that provided an element of surprise to shoppers. By 1991, when the program was discontinued, the stores had lost focus and were misusing the BlueLight Specials to unload defective merchandise or out-of-season clothing.

Ames stores copied the concept with an Amber Light Special in the '80s. Their copy-cat program was short lived.

Kmart revived the BlueLight Special in 2001, re-introducing it as "BlueLight Always." The new program was intended as a price war against Walmart. BlueLight Always, an attempt to go back to the company's roots, called for a special every hour on the hour. Each special lasted for 20 minutes. Only one product was featured on weekdays and two on weekends. All employees were required to stop what they were doing, clap twice, raise their fists in the air, and yell, "BlueLight, BlueLight."

The reinvention of the BlueLight program included painting bright blue stripes on the white store walls. A large hanging display that employees dubbed a "UFO" was actually an illuminated circle of royal blue fabric. The circle, measuring approximately 10 feet in circumference, was suspended from the ceiling. When the light was turned on, the new BlueLight Always logo was projected onto the floor and rotated.

A new stick figure mascot, still in use today, was designed to look like a walking, talking BlueLight man. The new BlueLight program was not totally carried out in all of the stores, due to understaffing and a lack of employee enthusiasm. Most employees hated the new program, and some would hide in the restroom to avoid participating. The program was discontinued again in 2002 when it was deemed non-productive.

BlueLight Always was briefly revived in 2005, and again four years later, on Saturdays only, with sales on selected merchandise lasting up to one hour. Kmart sold a limited edition BlueLight Special board game, which is a rare collectible item now available on Ebay.

The first time I ever shopped at Kmart 9000 was in the fall of 1974 when the store was new. I bought some baby clothes for 50 cents each on a BlueLight Special. At the time, I didn't know I would eventually become a Kmart employee. More than 16 years later, long after he outgrew those BlueLight clothes, my son became a Kmart employee, too.

I was known as the "BlueLight Queen" because I announced thousands of specials during my Kmart career.

A Family Affair

Several members of my family had worked at Murphy's, and Kmart became a family affair, too. Both of my sons worked at Kmart when they were in high school and college. Since the three of us were working at Kmart most evenings, my husband Randy decided to get a part-time evening job at the store so he could spend more time with his family.

The managers told me about every minor infraction that my family members committed. My younger son cut his hand with an "illegal" box cutter (a box cutter that was not issued by Kmart but was used by everyone because the approved ones were worthless). The cut was serious enough to require an emergency room visit and stitches. I was told that he cut his hand on purpose to get out of working because he was lazy.

An assistant manager once told my older son to get rid of his chewing gum. She held out her hand, so he complied by spitting the gum into her hand. Of course, she told me about it, and I just laughed and said that he had done exactly what she requested.

Randy had a headache one evening and was reprimanded for going into the breakroom to get some aspirin from the first aid kit. He didn't know employees were only allowed to get a headache while on break.

One evening an employee brought a Christmas necktie to me and said it had been found in the restroom. The necktie belonged to one of my sons, so I took it home and put it on the kitchen counter. When my son saw it, he told me the necktie had fallen in the toilet at Kmart, so he had just left it there. I decided to throw the tie away.

Both of my sons' wives worked briefly at Kmart, one at the service desk and one in the cafeteria. I often heard about their infractions, too.

I suggested getting a family photo taken at the Kmart Portrait Studio, with all of us wearing our red Kmart vests. That idea was very quickly voted down!

My granddaughter was born while we all worked at Kmart, so she was a "Kmart baby." Most of the employees showered her with attention, and she knew many of them by name when she was a toddler. I always thought she would work at Kmart when she grew up, but the store closed a couple of years before she turned 16. She worked at Pamida/ Shopko during summer breaks from high school.

In August of 2008, the Bryan Kmart signed a five-year lease. The store was spruced up with new paint and extensive cleaning. New tile, vents, and restroom counters were added. Plans were in place to revamp the electronics department and add to the product line. On February 27, 2009, the surprising announcement was made that Kmart 3960 would be closing its doors on May 24. The store was one of 24 Kmart locations closed for financial reasons.

Part of the building is now a Goodwill Store, and the rest is vacant. The former employees of Kmart 3960 meet for breakfast once a month and also reminisce at a potluck every year in November. There is also a Kmart 3960 group on Facebook.

Final Thoughts

I learned a lot during my long career in retail, including the popular slogan "Retail is detail." Times have changed a lot since I started working at Murphy's in 1973. Everyone seems to be in a hurry these days, and customers are often short on patience. Those types of customers were not as common when stores were smaller and easier to navigate.

Everyone should work in retail for at least a year or two. Some customers just look for things to complain about, whining if they are not helped in less than a minute. Hundreds of customers over the years told me something should be free if there was no price on it or the item would not scan.

Retail pays very low wages, but much is expected of the employees. At Kmart, we were timed on how fast we got customers through the checkout line. If it wasn't fast enough, we were reprimanded. The management didn't factor in customers who held up the line by running back to get another item or taking an excessive amount of time to pay for their purchases. My fellow Kmart employees figured out that we could "stop the timer" by locking our register during those delays.

Some people are extremely slow when writing a check, once they locate the checkbook and a pen. They usually ask what the date is, then the name of the store. The number of people who don't know what store they are in is mind-boggling. Do people really write checks anymore? The answer is yes, and they are always in line right ahead of me.

Other customers insist on paying with the exact change, right down to the last penny, even if they have to empty the contents of their purse on the counter to do so. It doesn't matter if there are ten people waiting in line behind them. I often get in line behind those people, too.

Cashiers are often required to ask every customer to buy an extended warranty, sign up for a store credit card, buy an add-on item, or donate a dollar to a charity. It is annoying for the customer and the cashier, but employees who don't comply with the store's policies are often reprimanded.

Most people believe the saying, "The customer is always right," and believe that their demands should always be met, no matter how absurd. Customers scream at store employees for things they have no control over.

Customers are often talking on their cell phones as they shop and are unable to stop talking long enough to speak to the cashier. I often wonder how people were able to shop before cell phones became popular. Customers even continue their conversations in the store's restroom, which makes me want to flush the toilet multiple times or make other noises.

I learned an important rule of retail while working at the service desk. The customer in front of you is more important than the one on the phone. The person who has made the effort to come into the store deserves your attention before a caller on the phone, who may or may not ever set foot inside the store.

The cash register will soon be obsolete. Many stores are starting to use smartphones, tablets, or iPads to ring up sales.

Everyone should experience retail from "the other side of the counter."

Acknowledgements

I would like to thank Joyce Yoder of the Williams County Public Library for her assistance with this book. She provided many of the photos of former stores in Bryan. Her research and sharing of newspaper articles proved invaluable to this project.

I would also like to thank Alan Benjamin for his assistance. He provided all of the photos of former stores in Montpelier. His research and sharing of his personal history files added a lot of invaluable information to this book. All of the photos of Trautman's store are from the Jim Trautman Collection.

Special thanks to Tim Tonjes for sharing information about stores in Defiance and Bryan and also some of his personal Kmart photos.

About the Author

Becky Corwin-Adams was born in Defiance, Ohio. Becky is a wife, a mother of two sons, and "MawMaw" to four grandchildren. She currently shares her home with seven cocker spaniels.

As a child, Becky had one cocker spaniel, dozens of cats, chickens, and a variety of "pocket pets." She started writing stories about her pets at an early age. Becky is a freelance writer and columnist for The Farmland News and the author of *Cast-Off Cocker Spaniels, Cherished Cats and Childhood Capers, Tails Along the Trails: Walking Adventures with Dogs, and Adventures of an Air Force Wife*. Becky volunteers for

Columbus Cocker Rescue as a foster parent, transporter, and Ebay seller.

Becky has been an avid reader since childhood. She especially enjoys reading Amish fiction, mysteries, and dog stories. When Becky isn't reading or writing, she enjoys crafting and walking with her cocker spaniels. She has had dozens of her original craft patterns published in various craft magazines.

You'll love these other books by Becky Corwin-Adams:

Adventures of an Air Force Wife

Cast-Off Cocker Spaniels

Cherished Cats and Childhood Capers

Tails Along the Trails: Walking Adventures with Dogs

ADVENTURES OF AN AIR FORCE WIFE
by Becky Corwin-Adams

The Adams' Air Force adventures take place in the '70s, in a time of CB radios, well before cell phones and the Internet. This true story begins at Chanute Air Force Base in Rantoul, Illinois, where the family of three lived in their first apartment, which featured an overflowing bathtub, a missing hamster, and some too-close neighbors.

Life became even more exciting when the young family was forced to leave the Midwest, their comfort zone, and relocate to cold, snowy Minot, North Dakota. With no home, no furniture, and little money, the Adams faced many unique challenges, like making ends meet on an airman's pay and keeping warm in a city whose slogan is appropriately, "Why not Minot? Freezin' is the reason. Ice is nice."

From dumpster diving to watching a baby entrusted to them by someone they met on a CB radio, the Adams' adventures go on and on as they make their way through life as a military family. If you have served our country or married someone who has, this book is for you!

CAST-OFF COCKER SPANIELS

by Becky Corwin-Adams

The perfect book for any Cocker Spaniel lover!

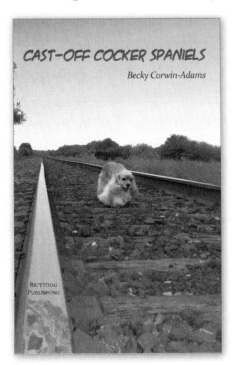

Excerpt: Nine-year-old Rags was found roaming the streets as a stray. When she landed at the shelter, she needed six baths to free her from the oil in which she was covered. Her little rear had no fur, and the skin in that area was as tough as leather. Her issues were severe, including water-filled blisters on her feet and legs.

Poor Rags was the saddest-looking Cocker I had ever seen. Her eyes were downcast and droopy, and the fur around them was gone. She certainly was not very attractive.

For many long months we treated Rags with antibiotics, and we bathed her three times a week with medicated shampoo. She was a good patient, never complaining even though she had to soak in the bathtub for 10 minutes each time.

Finally, our efforts paid off, and a new dog emerged. At adoption events, people commented on Rags' beauty and her soulful face. This was progress! Now, our task was to convince some special person to look beyond her age.

Does Rags find a home? Buy the book to find out! Proceeds from the book are donated back to cocker spaniel rescue.

Cherished Cats and Childhood Capers

by Becky Corwin-Adams

Life was never boring in Defiance, Ohio!

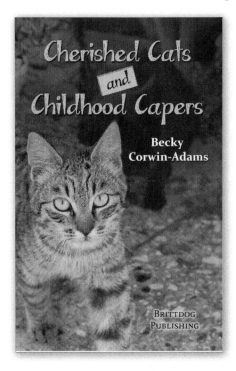

Cherished Cats
and
Childhood Capers

Becky
Corwin-Adams

BRITTDOG
PUBLISHING

Excerpt: "Our class went to the school library for a research project. As I was looking for a book, a note that was folded up like a football flew over the top of a six-foot-high bookshelf and landed at my feet. It was a request for my friend Cindy and me to go on a double date with Randy and his best friend, Tim.

The following day, a five-pound bag of sour balls mysteriously appeared in my locker, along with another note requesting a date. I found out where Randy's locker was and returned the candy, along with a note saying that Cindy and I had to work on Friday night, so we could not go on a date with them.

A day or two later, the persistent guys asked where we worked, and I told them we worked at Murphy's in Defiance. (I actually did work there, but Cindy didn't have a job.) I thought that was the end of them, until they showed up at Murphy's on Friday night and tried to talk to me while I was working. I didn't even know Randy's name yet. He had been signing the notes with his nickname, "Preacher Boy."

Randy found out where I lived, and on Good Friday, he dropped by my house unexpectedly. When I opened the door, my hair full of bright pink plastic curlers that were as large as orange juice cans, there he was, asking me to join him for a cruise through downtown Defiance..."

Did Randy's persistence pay off? Read the book to find out.

TAILS ALONG THE TRAILS: WALKING ADVENTURES WITH DOGS

by Becky Corwin-Adams

Walking with dogs is always an adventure!

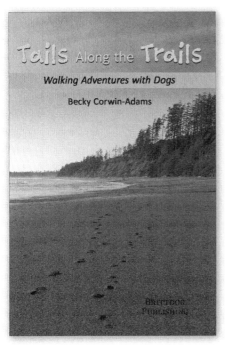

Becky Corwin-Adams and her husband, Randy, are members of a walking club, the American Volkssport Association. With the "help" of their dogs, they complete a 10-kilometer (six-mile) walk almost every weekend, but that's only the beginning of their walking adventures.

Be it in the city or on the trail, as a family with seven rescued cocker spaniels, the Adams walk a lot. In this book, you can join them on their journeys as they discover new places, have exciting adventures, and make lifelong friends.

The book details charity walks and volkswalks. The book explains volkssporting and contains information about the American Volkssport Association, an active world-wide walking organization. Volkssporting clubs are located in many cities in the United States, Canada, and dozens of other countries around the world.

The book includes walking adventures across the state of Ohio, many other states, and Canada. From star sightings while walking in Las Vegas, to attending national walking conventions, getting lost along the trail, and walking in all kinds of weather, walking is always an adventure, especially when accompanied by dogs!

The book includes more than 40 photos taken along the walking trails.

Made in the USA
Charleston, SC
14 March 2015